Written and compiled by Lois Rock
Illustrations copyright © 2003 Katherine Lucas
This edition copyright © 2003 Lion Publishing

The moral rights of the author and illustrator
have been asserted

Published by
Lion Publishing plc
Mayfield House, 256 Banbury Road,
Oxford OX2 7DH, England
www.lion-publishing.co.uk
ISBN 0 7459 4623 2

First edition 2003
10 9 8 7 6 5 4 3 2 1 0

All rights reserved

Acknowledgments
The extracts in this book have been inspired
by or adapted from the biblical verses noted
in each case, unless otherwise stated.
Bible extract on p. 22 quoted from the
Good News Bible published by The Bible
Societies/HarperCollins Publishers Ltd, UK
© American Bible Society 1966, 1971, 1976,
1992, used with permission.

A catalogue record for this book is available
from the British Library

Typeset in 14/16 Elegant Garamond BT
Printed and bound in Singapore

Little Blessings
FROM THE BIBLE

Lois Rock

Illustrated by Katherine Lucas

Good Things for You

May God bless you and take care of you.
May God be kind to you and do good
   things for you.
May God look on you with love and give
   you peace.

from Numbers 6:24–26

Those Who Do Right

God will bless those who do what is right,
those who say no to wrongdoing.
They will be like trees that grow beside
   a stream,
that stay green in the driest summer
and bear rich fruit at harvest time:
everything they do will go well.

from Psalm 1

Those Who Are Fair

Be fair to others and make this world
   a better place.
God will bless you.

If you see someone being treated unfairly,
   go to help them.
God will bless you.

If you see someone in need, share with
   them what you have.
God will bless you.

God's goodness will shine on you like
   the morning sun.

from Isaiah 58:6–8

Families

May God bless every family. May the children and the parents and the grandparents bring each other joy.

from Psalm 115:14

Children

Some people brought their children to Jesus.

He said a blessing prayer: 'Let the children come to me and do not stop them. The kingdom of heaven belongs to them.'

Jesus placed his hands on them as a sign of blessing, and then they went away.

from Matthew 19:13–15

Those Who Follow Jesus

May God give you all the good things that will help you to live as God's friends.

from Hebrews 13:20–21

Those Who Are Worried

God loves you, so don't let anything worry you or frighten you.

Daniel 10:18

God's Good Things

God will bless poor people:
the kingdom of God belongs to them.

God will bless those who go hungry:
God will fill them with good things.

from Luke 6:20–21

God's Great Reward

God will bless those who weep for sadness:
God will make them laugh for joy.

God will bless those who are bullied and
laughed at as they try to do what is right:
they can be happy inside, knowing that
they will have a great reward in heaven.

from Luke 6:21–23

Evening Blessing

Dear God,
This is my evening prayer:
Teach me to be careful in what I say.
Keep me from wanting to do wrong.
Keep me safe from every danger.

from Psalm 141